streets in public punishment. Princes and bishops were not immune; after one Archbishop of Canterbury died, his successor lasted just two days in London before he too succumbed. Across Europe, fearful people looked for scapegoats; they blamed the Jews, witches, foreigners, the people in the next town. In some places, terror bred horrific atrocities as Jews were burned in their houses for 'poisoning the wells'. England was spared such horrors, since its Jews had been expelled in 1290.

The bravest battled heroically to nurse the sick and dying, while others trudged stoically to and from gaping death-pits, their wagons and handcarts laden with blotched corpses. Many of the living abandoned their homes to flee. Crops stood unharvested, castles emptied, markets fell silent. Sheep and cattle 'went wandering over fields and through crops', falling into ditches with no one to 'drive or father them'. Death stalked country lanes and lay in wait at every street corner – until, as mysteriously as it had come, the pestilence departed. It left a lasting legacy, and questions surrounding its true nature, for medieval science found little to remark upon in rats and fleas and stinking open drains.

LEFT: *A 13th-century Persian painting shows the burial of a plague victim. The medicines of East and West could do little to check the remorseless spread of the Black Death.*

RIGHT: *Ghoulish plague images haunted Europe long after 1348. European doctors, like this German, masked and caped themselves against infection, looking more magical than medical.*

Cometh Catastrophe

In 1347, travellers returning from overseas carried the news of a mystery disease, blown, as it seemed, on the winds from China and central Asia. Early in 1348, England's king, Edward III, was with his army in France, consolidating the victory over the French at Crècy of a few months earlier, when reports of a terrible plague (the name Black Death came later) swept from the south. Thousands were dying in Italy; around 75 per cent of the citizens of Florence were dead, and 'many died daily or nightly in the public streets', recorded the writer Boccaccio. As the year passed, the plague spread fast, into Spain and southern France. No one was safe. The plague claimed two Spanish rulers, the Queen of Aragon and the King of Castile. On her way south to marry the prince of Castile, Edward III's daughter Joan died at Bordeaux in September 1348. Paris was in the grip of the terror during the summer of that year, and by August the first victims were dying in England.

The smitten English had, until that summer of 1348, been reasonably content. Edward III had recently defeated both Scots (at Neville's Cross) and French (at Crècy and Sluys) though war debts led the king to impose an extra tax on wool exports. To pay their taxes and put food in their bellies, the mass of England's people spent the summer working, as in previous summers, on the land … while catastrophe loomed.

BELOW: *Beggars await their turn to die in this fragment of a 14th-century Florence fresco* The Triumph of Death.

The English economy relied on farming and sheep-rearing for wool, but poor harvests in recent years had led to some belt-tightening amongst villagers. Almost 90 per cent of the people lived in villages, few with more than 400 inhabitants. London, the biggest city, held perhaps 70,000 people inside and close by its walls, their rubbish and sewage clogging small streams like the Fleet and causing even the Thames to stink. After Norwich (around 13,000 people) and York (10,000) there were few other large towns. When the Black Death struck, perhaps as many as 40 per cent of those citizens were soon buried in mass graves from which 'such a stench was given off that scarce anyone dared walk beside them', wrote William Dene, a monk of Rochester.

THE BLACK DEATH

The very name Black Death sends shivers up spines, summons up the worst nightmares. In the Middle Ages, the onset of this mysterious plague that killed millions of victims, many within a few hours, spread fear, panic and self-loathing. The Black Death struck Britain in 1348–49, and the foundations of feudal society were shaken. And yet society survived. Perhaps this is the ultimate hopeful message of a catastrophe now as much myth as history.

Just as deadly as the most cataclysmic natural disaster – volcano, flood, earthquake or hurricane – is that unseen killer, the deadly microbe. Society in the 21st century, with all its medical marvels, still quakes at the threat of mass destruction by germs, through terrorist-borne epidemic or missile-bearing biological warfare.

In the 14th century, germ-death came dancing out of Asia, and across Europe, leaving millions of corpses wherever it whirled. Against this peril medieval medicine was as powerless as medieval magic. 'Sometimes death came by road, passing from village to village, sometimes by river' – death in a most horrid and sudden form, striking down rich and poor, noble and peasant, priest and pauper, Muslim and Christian.

In 14th-century war-torn France, the plague carried off victorious English archers and demoralized French knights alike. In England, infection seeped through the stinking alleys of towns into gardens and great halls. It stalked the fields, leaving empty cottages and weed-choked fields. This was the great mortality, the pestilence, the Black Death.

The Church preached penitence, to seek pardon for God's wrath, and Christian people prayed for salvation, while some flogged themselves bloodily through the

THE RAT PROBLEM

The traditional villain in the Black Death story is the rat, or to be more precise the black rat *Rattus rattus* (it is thought brown or Norway rats did not reach Britain until the 1500s). Rats had fleas, and rats and fleas spread disease. The Black Death was, so the story went, probably bubonic plague, carried by fleas nestling in rats that scampered up and down the ropes of ships in port – the rats' revenge on human persecutors?

LEFT: *Infected with the plague bacillus, a hungry flea (here much magnified) was likely to infect humans with every bite.*

BELOW: *Travellers carried the disease from the East. This European painting purports to show visitors to Beijing.*

LONDON'S RANK RIVER

Summer was always the worst time for city smells. Edward III had complained of the state of London and its river, from which 'we have beheld dung and lay stools and other filth accumulated in diverse places within the city … and fumes and other abominable stenches …'. The king feared 'great peril to persons dwelling within the city'.

ABOVE RIGHT: *Death takes the priest; godly and ungodly alike were stricken. This image comes from a 15th-century French manuscript now in Lambeth Palace Library.*

AN AIRBORNE DISEASE?

The Kipchaks were Turkic-speaking people of central Asia. In 1347 their army was besieging the Genoese trade-fort of Kaffa in the Crimea. Suddenly Kipchak warriors began to sicken and die, swelling blackly and oozing blood. In an act of despairing inspiration (not uncommon in medieval warfare) those still standing had sufficient vengeful vitality to catapult rotting, diseased corpses over the walls. Thus the Genoese were infected, and when survivors from Kaffa sailed to Sicily, they carried the disease to Europe.

ABOVE: *In this pastoral idyll, medieval life looks happy, healthy and prosperous. Before and after 1348, sheep were key animals in the English economy.*

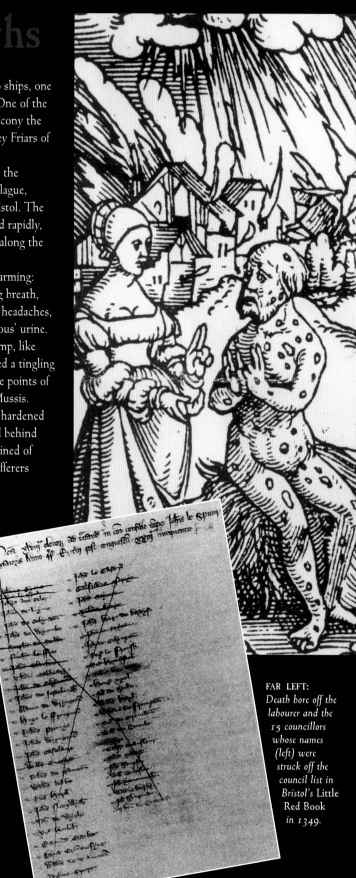

'In Melcombe [Weymouth, Dorset] two ships, one of them from Bristol, came alongside. One of the sailors had brought with him from Gascony the seeds of the terrible pestilence ....' So the Grey Friars of Lynn recorded the beginning of the horror.

Other places were also blamed, or received the dubious honour of being entry ports for the plague, among them Southampton, Plymouth and Bristol. The source mattered little, for the contagion spread rapidly, prompting the rich and able-bodied to escape along the dusty roads, taking infection with them.

The symptoms of the Black Death were alarming: a blackened tongue, vomiting, sweats, stinking breath, shortage of breath, dark blotches on the skin, headaches, loss of appetite, restlessness, 'foamy and odorous' urine. For most victims, the first sign was a small lump, like that caused by an insect bite. Sufferers reported a tingling sensation, 'as if they were being pricked by the points of arrows' according to the Italian Gabriele de' Mussis. There followed the 'boils', which swelled and hardened into painful 'buboes' in the groin, armpits and behind the ear. The patient became weak and complained of headaches. This was bubonic plague; some sufferers recovered but most died within a week.

FAR LEFT:
Death bore off the labourer and the 15 councillors whose names (left) were struck off the council list in Bristol's Little Red Book in 1349.

More virulent were two other forms of disease, affecting the lungs (pneumonic plague) and the blood (septicaemic plague). Those so infected died almost without exception, and within hours – three to four days at most. Medieval physicians, skilled at herb-potions and surgery for wounds sustained at work or in battle, were at a loss. One theory was that death was spread by an invisible poisonous mist, conjured up by an unfortunate conjunction of the planets – and against such a calamity, there was no potion or plaster, spell or charm in the apothecary's cupboard nor even in the alchemist's cabinet.

THE PLAGUE PUZZLE

Within eight months the Black Death had spread south to north through Britain, a frightening rate of transmission. Towns were worst affected, but in the course of ten or so weeks, a village could lose half its population. Yet modern studies have shown that bubonic plague is not very contagious from person to person. So what was the Black Death? And were rats, or their fleas, to blame?

ABOVE: *The Black Death came into Britain through the ports, in ships carrying traders and (as here) pilgrims, regular travellers on Europe's wandering highways and coastal sea routes.*

7

Fear, Flight and Fantasy

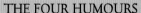

RIGHT: *St Roch, a French holy man said to have cured Black Death victims in Italy. Others prayed to him for a miracle cure. When Roch fell ill, a dog brought him bread to aid his recovery. Here the saint points to the dreaded plague buboe on his thigh.*

Medieval people were accustomed to death, but this was a death of shocking, if merciful, speed. 'Those who fell sick of a kind of gross swelling of the flesh lasted for barely two days …' reported John of Fordun, a monk of Aberdeen. Within a few hours, healthy men and women were transformed into pock-marked corpses. Mortality rates were terrifyingly high, around 50 per cent, far higher than in modern outbreaks of bubonic plague. The Black Death killed as readily in cold weather as in summer – another fact that has made some puzzled modern researchers question the rat-flea-death link, since rat fleas are supposedly less active in winter. Nor do hordes of rats, alive or dead, figure in the medieval accounts, though some archaeological evidence, from rat bones at human sites, suggests that in some English port-towns, at least, the rat population was exploding.

The medieval theory of humours (see panel left) could not account for, nor vanquish, such a fearful killer. Was the Black Death a combination of bubonic and pneumonic plague, together with a cocktail of other diseases including smallpox, dysentery and assorted fevers? A more recent theory suggests not bubonic plague at all, but a viral infection, a haemorrhagic fever causing internal and external bleeding,

ABOVE: *A window panel in All Saints' Church, North Street, York, shows plague victims on their deathbeds, while a leering Death awaits.*

ABOVE: *The dead rise up. In this 1604 engraving, gravediggers flee from the opening graves of medieval Black Death victims, supposedly buried while still alive.*

directly transmitted and usually fatal, but to which a minority of people had a natural immunity, built up over many centuries and perhaps originating in Mesopotamia or the Nile Valley. Whatever the epidemic may have been, it was deadly – and for all people knew at the time, everyone might die.

In desperation, the living turned to charms, potions, and cure-alls. It was suggested that people living in low-built houses were safer from the 'miasma' in the air, as were those with north-facing windows; it was best to keep south-facing windows shut. Burning aromatic woods, such as juniper, would 'purify' the air, and sniffing the fumes of frankincense, marjoram, tamarisk and aloe was also recommended. The aid of concerned saints in heaven, such as St Roch, should be invoked through prayer. The best advice from one of Europe's most learned institutions, the University of Paris, was to run, to get far away from places where the air was 'corrupted by vapours' – and that is what many did.

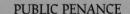

PUBLIC PENANCE

Flagellants paraded through towns in Germany and Flanders, whipping themselves with iron-tipped scourges until the blood ran. Such public acts of penance, the flagellants believed, might bring pardon for human sins and so avert the ultimate catastrophe – the end of the world.

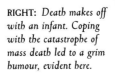

RIGHT: *Death makes off with an infant. Coping with the catastrophe of mass death led to a grim humour, evident here.*

Magic and Medicine

octors were largely helpless, since medieval science could neither understand nor treat an epidemic which spread at the rate of up to 8 kilometres (5 miles) a day. Most treatments were of limited value. The medieval doctrine of humours led to some patients being 'bled' (to remove unwholesome humours from the body), which only weakened them further. Nor was fasting as a sign of moral repentance likely to help a failing patient.

Many people put their trust in charms, spells and incantations, at the same time swallowing whatever potion the local quack or 'wise woman' recommended. Practical steps might be taken. Some doctors advised cleanliness, and believed that gardens were healthier than streets, since sweet smells were good against the 'noxious air'. On the other hand, some thought that breathing in even more noxious airs, from the privy, might do you good – fighting fire with fire, as it were. Herbs were a mainstay of medieval medicine, and suggestions too for healthy drinking included adding sage, rue and rose water to drinks.

A doctor takes a no-nonsense approach, attacking his patient's plague buboes with a knife, to cut out the infection. This woodcut dates from the 1400s.

ABOVE: *No doubt most folk held their breath while in a privy, but some physicians claimed that bad smells were effective against plague.*

A POET'S ADVICE
The English poet John Lydgate (1370–c.1451) wrote *A Diet and Doctrine for the Pestilence*, in which he warned against excessive indulgence of any type. 'Especially make not visits to brothels and baths,' he said.

ABOVE: *Most gardeners grew herbs, much used in medieval medicine, and the sweet smells of flowers were thought beneficial to people seeking to protect themselves from infection.*

Doctors were better at marking the passage of symptoms than in treating the disease. They recorded that as death drew nearer, the patient's skin colour darkened and the face grew blotchy and of a greenish hue. It was noted that 'stinking sweat is a matter of concern', also stinking vomit, either the green like a leek leaf 'or the red darkened with blackness'.

The Italians, belatedly, imposed quarantine regulations on ships from Eastern ports. Doctor Michele Savonarola, who in the 1340s worked at the ducal court at Ferrara, took careful notes of the disease's progress. He remarked that 'when the patient appears to be greatly weakened, and to have lost all strength … then there is clear reason to believe that it is pestilential fever.' The patient was put to bed, the house sealed, the relatives standing by, waiting.

RIGHT: *Death persuades a reluctant friar to join him: another lively cameo from the 15th-century French manuscript in Lambeth Palace.*

The Great Mortality

'Sometimes it stops in some places, or lessens, but it is never really gone. Just when it seems to be over, it returns and attacks once more those who were briefly happy,' wrote the Italian poet Petrarch in 1367. He had lost his adored muse Laura to the plague in 1348. Further outbreaks haunted Europe for a generation, for the Black Death cast a long shadow. Perhaps 20 million Europeans died from it.

Within a year, Britain's population was reduced by up to a third. For England, much the largest nation in Britain, this suggests a death toll of around 1.3 million. Hundreds of villages were left desolate, and some were abandoned for ever after the 'great mortality'. With entire households dying within days, fields were left without ploughmen, hayfields without men to mow them, sheep without shepherds. Mills, forges and shops were closed. People lived in dread of strangers. The cleric Geoffrey le Baker described how the people of Gloucester 'refused those of Bristol entrance' for fear that 'their breath would be infectious'. Henry Knighton, another chronicler, reported that many sheep also died 'and so rotted that neither beast nor bird would touch them'.

The year of the pestilence 'cleared many country villages entirely of every human being'. In November 1348 the plague reached London where, according to the chronicler Robert of Avesbury, more than 200 bodies were buried daily in the new cemetery hurriedly opened near Smithfield. In January 1349 the English Parliament

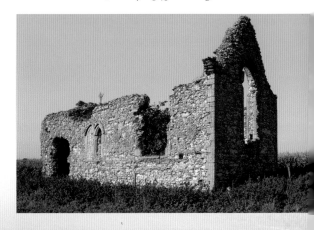

ABOVE: *Villages emptied, and some were never restored to former vitality. Churches fell into disrepair, like this one at Ringstead Parva, near Hunstanton in Norfolk.*

ABOVE: *The mark of pestilence. Necrosis of tissue (gangrene), caused by pneumonic plague.*

Middle Ditchford in Gloucestershire, a village no more. From the air the pattern of medieval lanes and fields can still be traced more than 600 years after the Black Death caused the old village to be abandoned.

was suspended for the safety of the great and good now fled to the shires. Two former Chancellors of England died, as did many merchants and up to 40 per cent of the clergy. Between a third and half of London's population of around 70,000 godly and godless souls died before the plague subsided in the spring of 1349.

As the graveyards filled, fields were opened as burial grounds, and mass graves dug for corpses. Parents buried children, children buried parents. The economic impact was considerable. Seaford in Sussex was said in 1356 to be still so 'desolated by plague' that the few survivors were unable to pay their taxes or defend the town. The village of Tusmore in Oxfordshire was one of those communities that 'died': its fields were turned into a park because by 1358 there were no longer any taxpayers. Middle Ditchford in Gloucestershire was another 'lost village'. Once thronged with over 1,000 inhabitants, it was abandoned, its streets and lanes overgrown, its strip fields given over to grazing.

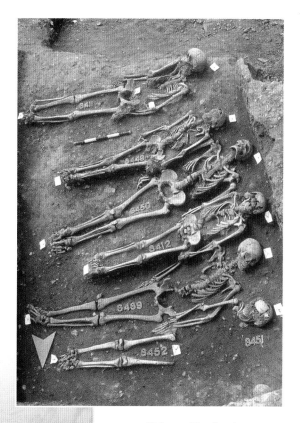

ABOVE: *Skeletons of London plague victims found at Smithfield. Here, burials were orderly, with bodies stacked like bottles in a wine rack.*

ABOVE: *Mass burials at Tournai in Flanders. Gravediggers work grimly while mourners carry a procession of coffins including those of children.*

13

The Rootless Phantom

With so many dead, and dying, it is hardly surprising that reactions varied from resigned apathy to all-out frenzy. Not even the godly within walls were safe. At Michelham Priory, just north of modern Eastbourne in Sussex, eight out of thirteen brothers died. So did the Abbot of Battle Abbey, despite the recent additions to the abbey's moat and ramparts, designed to keep out invaders. 'We see death coming into our midst like black smoke … a rootless phantom which has no mercy for fair countenance …' wrote the Welsh poet Ieuan Gethin.

Graveyards became so full that disputes arose between clergy and people. The Church insisted that the dead be buried in consecrated ground, to await Resurrection Day, while some of the populace clamoured for the death-carts to trundle beyond the town walls. Death-pits were soon places to avoid, because of the stench arising from too-hasty burials. The Bishop of Winchester called for public shows of penance and issued stern warnings that his flock must avert their eyes (and divert their bodies) from sin. It did no good; perhaps half of Winchester's population, then probably around 10,000, were soon dead, among them over half the Bishop's clergy.

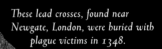

These lead crosses, found near Newgate, London, were buried with plague victims in 1348.

William Dene of Rochester ranted that 'the entire population has become more depraved'. The establishment was particularly concerned that workmen, skilled and unskilled, showed signs of being 'carried away by the spirit of revolt'. But by and large, law and order were maintained. Medieval people were accustomed to death. When the plague struck, relatives made sure the dying victim saw a priest, if possible, and then made a will.

In August 1349, William Needler of York died. It was just one more death, but there was an inquest – perhaps because a neighbour was suspicious. Despite the plague raging in the city, a jury was found, evidence heard, and the verdict pronounced: death from natural causes, 'by reason of the pestilence'. A small triumph for normality, in the face of bewildering catastrophe.

LEFT: Michelham Priory, East Sussex, suffered badly in the Black Death. More than half of its small religious community died of plague.

aonis tuc lep brticfiu
a femp iucuuat · p ·
Tauilla pmoztate boim oñ

s qui nõ moztē
penitntiaã uc

ABOVE: The consolation of the Church. This illustration from a manuscript in the Bodleian Library, Oxford, shows a tonsured priest celebrating Mass for ailing Black Death sufferers.

ABOVE: Medieval sorcery – a severed hand being used in magical healing. The Church, medicine and magic were rivals in the battle against the Black Death.

MARKS OF DEATH

Gethin the poet left a vivid description of the dreaded buboes under the arms; describing them as 'of the form of an apple, like the head of an onion ... great is its seething, like a burning cinder, a grievous thing of an ashy colour.' A healthy look and 'fair countenance' were no defence against the onset of the marks of death.

God's Wrath

The fate of those in the next village was often of little interest to the pitiful victims, their distraught families, and those still fit enough to struggle on with the essential everyday tasks. 'Try to be happy and avoid sadness entirely' was a heartening, if hardly appropriate, health tip. However, most preventive suggestions concentrated on bodily precautions, such as 'when rising early, do so with the aid of a fire … avoid hot baths … have nothing to do with older sensual women'. Most doctors advocated a sensible moderation, especially in eating and drinking. No fruit, poultry rather than red meat, plenty of sauces and spices, only 'wholesome wine and white bread'.

Prayer, the habit of the devout and the last resort of the worldly-wise, seemed the only hope of salvation from the scything progress of the pestilence. Preachers railed against vice and greed, calling on the faithful to mend their ways. Some hailed the imminent end of the world. Although some clergy deserted their flocks or retreated within monastery walls, many priests and monks worked heroically to give comfort to the stricken, and the last rites to the dying. Westminster Abbey's south cloister contains a slab thought to cover the remains of the Abbot and 27 of his monks. Deaths among English clergy were higher than the average toll, and church records painstakingly kept by monks, often ill themselves, are an important source of data for modern historians.

Northern English cities such as Newcastle and Carlisle were not only 'wasted' by disease, but were also threatened by the Scots who 'rejoicing thought they would obtain all they wished' – until they too felt the edge of the 'sword of the anger of God' (Geoffrey le Baker). Convinced that the Black Death was God's just punishment for English sins, they saw their chance to aid divine retribution, and attacked Durham in 1349. But the scourge was impartial, and by 1350 Scots were dying as readily as English. Death 'showed favour to no one', commented Robert of Avesbury.

RIGHT: *For many sufferers, prayer seemed the only hope, for this life or the next.*

BELOW: *The Church had a long association with the plague. Here Pope Gregory the Great seeks divine intervention against a 6th-century outbreak in Rome.*

ABOVE: *The Church used all its forces to fight the pestilence. In Tournai, Belgium, in 1090, relics of the Virgin Mary were carried through streets filled with the dying and the desperate. Similar measures were tried in the 1340s.*

PLAGUE HITS THE CHURCH

The plague obliged the Church to relax some rules. The Bishop of Lincoln gave every priest the power to hear confession and absolve the dying from their sins 'except in matters of debt' (the dying man or his relatives were urged to pay the debt). Religious faith was shaken and religious building interrupted by shortage of labour. Work at the cathedrals of York, Exeter, Lichfield and Winchester was stopped, then restarted – though the scaffolding remained standing at Winchester until after 1370, with little new work done.

Survival

The pestilence hit Wales, Scotland and Ireland (though records for these countries are less detailed than for England). In Ireland, according to the chronicler Geoffrey le Baker, it first killed the English settlers, sparing the 'pure Irish who lived amongst the mountains' until 1357, when they too began to die.

By 1355 the worst seemed to be over for England. Normal life began to resume, with trade and travel, and people returned to pick up the pieces. The living took over the tenancies of the dead, and the seasonal pattern of rural life was restored, even in villages now only a

third their pre-plague size. Many monasteries were half-empty, their monks lying in quiet graves, yet new churches and chantry chapels were built. Prayers of thanksgiving and masses for the souls of the departed were mingled with prayers that no such calamity should return. But return it did – in renewed outbreaks during the later 1300s, and into succeeding centuries.

For some at least there was a silver lining. Death's scythe left a labour shortage, so that the peasant, carpenter and mason could demand a higher wage for his hire, and lower rents. Prices fell, and in the new economic climate, the rising survivors found a profit,

BELOW: *The Dance of Death. In the wake of the catastrophe, artists became obsessed with skeletal imagery, and visions of human mortality.*

ABOVE: *The Statute of Labourers reflected the new economic climate following the Black Death.*

and uncertainty. The 'Dance of Death' fascinated artists, who painted grinning skulls and dancing skeletons. Tombs were decorated with grisly worm-eaten corpses beneath – and often in place of – robed and reposing bishops, knights and ladies. Death the peace-giver had become Death the destroyer of dignity. 'Foul and stinking is my rotting' as one poet put it. Cynicism and moral laxity, living for the moment, were unexpected consequences, which alarmed moralists. The cleric Robert Rypon of Durham blamed this on French fashions; the poet William Langland wrote that post-plague marriages were doomed, their 'only fruit is foul words'.

ABOVE: *After its onslaught in 1348, the plague returned to strike Britain again. Anne of Bohemia, queen of King Richard II of England, was a victim of an outbreak in 1394.*

increasing their land-holdings and building stone cottages to replace the wood and mud dwellings they had known as children. In 1351 the king introduced a new law, the Statute of Labourers, in an attempt to fix rents and wages, but market forces pushed them up regardless. An awakening peasantry had discovered new economic muscle, encouraging the protests that led to the Peasants' Revolt of 1381. The terrible plague had played its part in hastening a gradual change from feudalism to capitalism.

The Black Death was not the end of the world, but it definitely did seem to mark a watershed, ending a golden age of chivalry and faith, and casting mankind into doubt

THE PLAGUE AND LINGUISTIC CHANGE

After the Black Death, English, rather than Latin or French, became the language of government. Teachers taught pupils to translate from Latin to English, rather than into French. In 1363, Parliament was opened in English. Wycliffe's English Bible appeared about 1382. A will made in English, the first of its kind, is known from 1387. The change may reflect the high losses among monkish scholars, a mood of anti-clericalism, a new nationalism, and a breaking down of old feudal barriers. Or perhaps too many French tutors had died.

Causes and Effects

Most scientists have believed the Black Death to be bubonic plague. This was claimed in the 1830s to be caused by poisoned air released by volcanoes, but was later attributed to rat-borne fleas. Biologists in the 1890s identified the bacillus, known since 1971 as *Yersina pestis* after the Swiss-French scientist Alexandre Yersin (1863–1943) who studied it in China, using corpses brought to him by British sailors stationed in Hong Kong.

The bacillus was linked with the black rat *Rattus rattus* and the rat-flea *Xenopsylla cheopis*. Bacillus-infected fleas build up in isolated rat populations (which acquire immunity), then jump to other rat colonies (without immunity) living close to humans. As rat-hosts die, hungry fleas bite humans. The plague bacillus resists attack from the human immune system and by reproducing extremely rapidly, overwhelms the body in a short time.

Although other diseases such as smallpox and malaria were major killers in the Middle Ages, the Black Death created its own macabre mystique. In Europe, the final death-toll was at least 25 million. Outbreaks recurred,

THE PANDEMIC THREAT

The modern world is not immune from collapse into fear and confusion – as witness the catastrophic floods that hit New Orleans in 2005. Pandemics remain a threat to civilized and largely antiseptic urban living, be it from 'avian flu' carried by migratory birds or the old enemy: the millions of rats that lurk in our sewers and subways. The 1906 San Francisco earthquake released thousands of rats from the sewers into the streets. A new Black Death might have ensued, had not the city residents killed the rats at a rate of 13,000 a week.